DOG BREEDS

Basset
Hounds

by Sara Green

Consultant:
Michael Leuthner, D.V.M.
Petcare Animal Hospital
Madison, Wisc.

BLASTOFF!
4
READERS

BELLWETHER MEDIA · MINNEAPOLIS, MN

Note to Librarians, Teachers, and Parents:

Blastoff! Readers are carefully developed by literacy experts and combine standards-based content with developmentally appropriate text.

Level 1 provides the most support through repetition of high-frequency words, light text, predictable sentence patterns, and strong visual support.

Level 2 offers early readers a bit more challenge through varied simple sentences, increased text load, and less repetition of high-frequency words.

Level 3 advances early-fluent readers toward fluency through increased text and concept load, less reliance on visuals, longer sentences, and more literary language.

Level 4 builds reading stamina by providing more text per page, increased use of punctuation, greater variation in sentence patterns, and increasingly challenging vocabulary.

Level 5 encourages children to move from "learning to read" to "reading to learn" by providing even more text, varied writing styles, and less familiar topics.

Whichever book is right for your reader, Blastoff! Readers are the perfect books to build confidence and encourage a love of reading that will last a lifetime!

This edition first published in 2011 by Bellwether Media, Inc.

No part of this publication may be reproduced in whole or in part without written permission of the publisher. For information regarding permission, write to Bellwether Media, Inc., Attention: Permissions Department, 5357 Penn Avenue South, Minneapolis, MN 55419.

Library of Congress Cataloging-in-Publication Data
Green, Sara, 1964–
  Basset hounds / by Sara Green.
    p. cm. — (Blastoff! readers. Dog breeds)
  Includes bibliographical references and index.
  Summary: "Simple text and full-color photographs introduce beginning readers to the characteristics of the dog breed Basset Hounds. Developed by literacy experts for students in kindergarten through third grade"–Provided by publisher.
  ISBN 978-1-60014-564-3 (hardcover : alk. paper)
  1. Basset hound–Juvenile literature. I. Title.
SF429.B2G74 2011
636.753'6–dc22
                                    2010034481

Printed in the United States of America, North Mankato, MN.
010111   1176

Contents

What Are Basset Hounds?

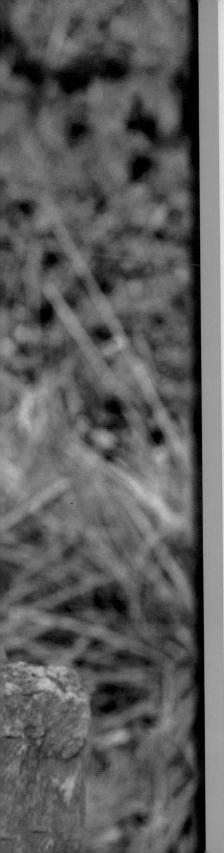

Basset Hounds are **sturdy** dogs with long bodies and short legs. They are often called Bassets. They are known for their sad-looking eyes.

Adult Basset Hounds are 12 to 14 inches (30 to 36 centimeters) tall at the shoulder. They weigh 45 to 65 pounds (20 to 29 kilograms).

Basset Hounds have smooth, short **coats** that come in a variety of colors. Many Basset Hounds have coats that are a mix of black, white, and tan. These are called **tri-color** coats.

Basset Hounds have large front paws that turn outward to help them keep their balance.

! fun fact

Basset Hounds have heavier bones than any other small dog breed. That's why Basset Hounds weigh so much for their size.

Basset Hounds are **scent hounds**. They are built to **track** scents. Their long ears often brush the ground when they walk.

This stirs up smells from the ground. Their loose, hanging **flews** and **dewlaps** help catch and bring the smells closer to their noses.

flew

dewlap➜

History of Basset Hounds

St. Hubert Hound

The Basset Hound **breed** is originally from France. Its **ancestor** was the St. Hubert Hound, a large hunting dog with long ears and an excellent sense of smell. People used St. Hubert Hounds to track deer and other animals.

fun fact

Most Basset Hounds have white tips on their tails. This helps people find them when they are hunting.

Some people wanted a shorter hound breed to track rabbits under brush. They chose the St. Hubert Hounds with the shortest legs to have puppies together.

These puppies had short legs, long ears, and a great sense of smell. They were the first Basset Hounds.

Basset Hounds were slow and steady walkers. They could track rabbits over long distances.

Basset Hounds were eventually brought to the United States. The gentle and friendly nature of Basset Hounds made them good **companion dogs**. People began keeping them as pets.

! fun fact

Basset Hounds have the second-strongest sense of smell of any dog breed. Only the Bloodhound has a stronger one.

Basset Hounds Today

Today, Basset Hounds still enjoy activities where they can use their sense of smell. Many Basset Hounds participate in **field trials**.

In a field trial, a rabbit runs through a field. A Basset Hound uses its sense of smell to follow the rabbit's scent trail. The Basset Hound earns points for how well it follows the scent trail.

Basset Hounds also use their sense of smell in **tracking trials**. In a tracking trial, a person walks away from a Basset Hound and drops items along the way. The Basset Hound tracks the person's scent to find each item. If it follows the scent trail, it will find the person at the end!

! fun fact
The French word *bas* means "low."

Basset Hounds also enjoy everyday
activities like going on walks and playing
with their owners. They love to explore
outside with their noses.

You never know what you might find when you take a walk with a Basset Hound!

Glossary

ancestor—a family member who lived long ago

breed—a type of dog

coats—the hair or fur of animals

companion dogs—dogs that provide friendship to people

dewlaps—the loose folds of skin that hang below the necks of some dogs

field trials—events where dogs test their skill at tracking small animals such as birds or rabbits

flews—loose, hanging lips

scent hounds—dogs that are bred for their ability to track smells

sturdy—having a strong, muscular body

track—to follow the trail of an animal or person

tracking trials—events that test a dog's ability to use its sense of smell to find a person; the dog must follow a trail of items with the person's scent.

tri-color—having three colors; tri-color dog coats are often black, white, and tan.

To Learn More

AT THE LIBRARY

American Kennel Club. *The Complete Dog Book for Kids*. New York, N.Y.: Howell Book House, 1996.

Gray, Susan H. *Basset Hounds*. Chanhassen, Minn.: Child's World, 2007.

Swaim, Jessica. *The Hound from the Pound*. Cambridge, Mass.: Candlewick Press, 2007.

ON THE WEB

Learning more about Basset Hounds is as easy as 1, 2, 3.

1. Go to www.factsurfer.com.

2. Enter "Basset Hounds" into the search box.

3. Click the "Surf" button and you will see a list of related Web sites.

With factsurfer.com, finding more information is just a click away.

Index